CLASSIC DUETS

9 TIMELESS FAVORITES FOR ONE PIANO, FOUR HANDS

Arranged by Phillip Keveren

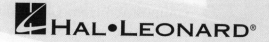

— PIANO LEVEL —
INTERMEDIATE

ISBN 978-1-70513-101-5

Visit Hal Leonard Online at
www.halleonard.com

Visit Phillip at
www.phillipkeveren.com

Contact us:
Hal Leonard
7777 West Bluemound Road
Milwaukee, WI 53213
Email: info@halleonard.com

In Europe, contact:
Hal Leonard Europe Limited
42 Wigmore Street
Marylebone, London, W1U 2RN
Email: info@halleonardeurope.com

In Australia, contact:
Hal Leonard Australia Pty. Ltd.
4 Lentara Court
Cheltenham, Victoria, 3192 Australia
Email: info@halleonard.com.au

PREFACE

We pianists spend a great deal of our practice time in isolation. The piano is an orchestra unto itself, and there is a lot of joy in playing an instrument for which mountains of solo repertoire has been composed. But, collaboration at the keyboard is a welcome diversion from solitary musical expression.

This collection brings together titles that seem to invite a duet approach. "A Bicycle Built for Two" speaks for itself, as does "Tea for Two"! "Chopsticks" and "Heart and Soul" are the bread and butter of many an impromptu piano-fest – arranged here for a more formal recital setting. "Two for the Road" has a perfect title for duet partners, and also happens to be one of my favorite Henry Mancini compositions.

So, I hope you will share the bench with a friend and enjoy these duet settings!

Sincerely,

Phillip Keveren

BIOGRAPHY

Phillip Keveren, a multi-talented keyboard artist and composer, has composed original works in a variety of genres from piano solo to symphonic orchestra. Mr. Keveren gives frequent concerts and workshops for teachers and their students in the United States, Canada, Europe, Australia, and Asia. He holds a B.M. in composition from California State University Northridge and a M.M. in composition from the University of Southern California.

CONTENTS

A BICYCLE BUILT FOR TWO
(Daisy Bell)

Words and Music
HARRY DAC
Arranged by Phillip Kever

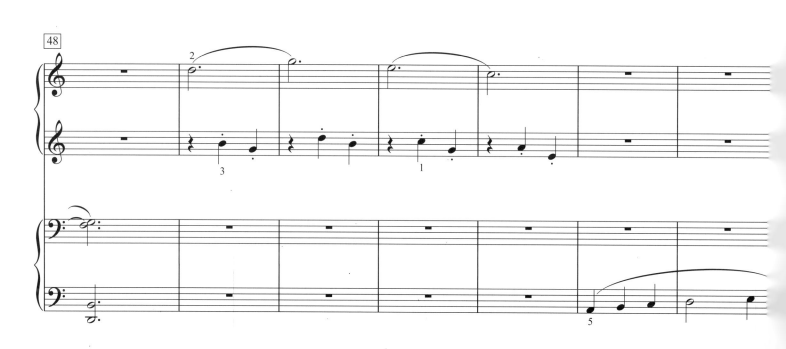

7

CHOPSTICKS

By ARTHUR DE LULLI
Arranged by Phillip Keveren

DO-RE-MI
from THE SOUND OF MUSIC

Lyrics by OSCAR HAMMERSTEIN
Music by RICHARD RODGE
Arranged by Phillip Kever

SILLY LOVE SONGS

Words and Music by PAUL McCARTNEY
and LINDA McCARTNEY
Arranged by Phillip Keveren

19

HEART AND SOUL
from the Paramount Short Subject A SONG IS BORN

Words by FRANK LOESSE
Music by HOAGY CARMICHAE
Arranged by Phillip Kevere

LEAN ON ME

Words and Music by
BILL WITHERS
Arranged by Phillip Keveren

SCARBOROUGH FAIR/CANTICLE

Arrangement and Original Counter Melody by
PAUL SIMON and ARTHUR GARFUNKEL
Arranged by Phillip Keveren

TEA FOR TWO
from NO, NO, NANETTE

Words by IRVING CAESAR
Music by VINCENT YOUMANS
Arranged by Phillip Keveren

TWO FOR THE ROAD

from TWO FOR THE ROAD

Music by HENRY MANCINI
Words by LESLIE BRICUSSE
Arranged by Phillip Keveren

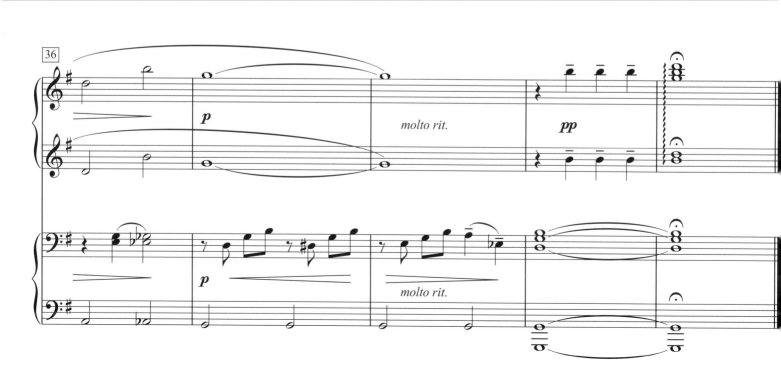